From the Valley to Victory

Audrey Pearl Williams

This book is a work of non-fiction, with ideas and events recalled from the author's memory. However, names have been changed for many of the individuals to protect their identities.

CLF Publishing, LLC.
9161 Sierra Ave, Ste. 203C
Fontana, CA 92335
www.clfpublishing.org
909.315.3161

Copyright © 2017 by Audrey Pearl Williams. All rights reserved. No portion of this book may be reproduced, stored in a retrieval system, or transmitted by any form or any means electronically, photocopied, recorded, or any other except for brief quotations in printed reviews, without the prior permission of the publisher.

Cover Design by Senir Design. Contact information- info@senirdesign.com.

ISBN # 978-1-945102-18-9

Printed in the United States of America.

Dedications

This book is lovingly dedicated to both my parents, with special love to Daddy, Troy Bradford.

And, to my children, who are very dear to me (tough love): Maurice, Sheritta, Shetona, Victor, and Hiawatha Jr.

Acknowledgements

I take this opportunity to acknowledge those who were instrumental in my Christian journey:
My eldest sister, LeeVada Cruthird (known as Mother Cre),
My sister Alfrida,
Dad Shumate,
Pastor Lollis,
and
Bishop Leon Martin.

Also, I acknowledge my publisher,
Dr. Cassundra White-Elliott, at CLF Publishing, LLC,
for her assistance in fulfilling this assignment.

Table of Contents

Chapter One: *Valley Life* — 9

Chapter Two: *Marriage and Motherhood* — 19

Chapter Three: *Single* — 25

Chapter Four: *Regrouping* — 31

Chapter Five: *Family Life* — 41

Chapter Six: *Church* — 53

Chapter Seven: *Disruption of Marriage* — 59

Chapter Eight: *Actualization* — 65

Chapter Nine: *Social Life* — 69

Chapter Ten: *Submission* — 79

About the Author — 85

Introduction

Life can be a bumpy road on which to travel, and it can lead you down paths you never imagined would surface in your life. However, if you submit yourself to a higher power, namely the Lord Jesus Christ, He will order your steps and place you on a road to success, victory, and even recovery (if need be). He will heal your wounds, and most importantly, He will give you wisdom when you need to make decisions that may impact your life as well as the lives of your family members (your mate and your children).

Life can also present a variety of choices, for which you need to make decisions. Sometimes the choices can be confusing and even daunting, while others may seem liberating. Regardless of what leads you to make a particular choice, it is the end result that really matters. One wrong choice and your life may be impacted forever!

My life was a seeming endless journey through a valley, in which I experienced joy, happiness, turmoil, pain, confusion, brokenness, and eventually, victory, when I made it to the end of the road. From a child, I had dreams, aspirations, and desires. However, what lie ahead for me in my immediate future was something I could not fathom, but it became my reality.

Later, I was able to live through the disparity and eventually find light at the end of the tunnel. As God says in the Holy Bible, "*I will never leave you nor forsake you.*" And as only God can, He held true to the very end!

In this book, **From the Valley to Victory**, I share my journey of *unexpected* occurrences and *expected* pleasures, so that you may have hope and an expected end. In Jeremiah 29:11, it says, "*For I know the thoughts that I think toward you, saith the Lord, thoughts of peace, and not of evil, to give you an expected end.*" God wants the best for us. We may not be able to see the light at the end of the tunnel, and the devil may attempt to steal our joy, but James said in Chapter 1:2-4, *"My brethren, **count it all joy** when ye fall into divers temptations; Knowing this, that the trying of your faith worketh patience. But let patience have her perfect work, that ye may be perfect and entire, wanting nothing."*

In all that you do, allow the Holy Ghost to be your guide. He will lead you to victory!

Chapter One
Valley Life

Children are born all times of the year and under different circumstances. Some in cold weather, while others in warm, sunny or hot weather. Some to single mothers or to happily married couples. For me, Audrey Pearl, well I was born during the very hot summer of August 1943 on the 27th day, in Merced, California. For my wonderful parents Troy and Ella Bradford, I was their fifth child. My stay in Merced, however, would prove to be brief because soon after my birth, my family and I moved to Madera, California. The exact time frame the move took place I'm not quite sure. I was a bit too young to remember. However, I do know we moved to a three-room house at 324 Hull Street. Our home consisted of a bedroom, a living room, and a kitchen. Even though there were quite a few people living in the three-room house, it was just fine for me. I had a normal and happy childhood.

My father, who worked construction, was the breadwinner of the family. As a result of his hard work and commitment to providing for his family, I always had lunch money, school clothes, a roof over my head, and food in my stomach. At five years old, I started school and attended kindergarten at Persia Elementary school. That was an exciting time in my life.

And, just like any other child, I got into my share of mischief. I remember eating mulberries from the trees, even when I was forbidden by my mother. The mulberries colored my mouth and would give me away each and every time. My mother would question me about my activity, and I would deny it. But, of course, she knew better.

After attending Persia Elementary for about a year, Sierra Vista Elementary School was built, and all of the children were transferred over because Persia was being torn down. Sierra Vista was further away from home, and we had to cross a field to get to it, but it was a new school, and all the students, including me, were ecstatic.

By the third grade, I had grown very comfortable with being in a school environment, so I began to increase my activities outside the classroom. I decided to expand my horizons, by gaining a job in the school cafeteria. I enjoyed my job immensely, and it gave me a sense of responsibility, which made me very proud. During that same time frame, I remember getting a new Schwinn bicycle. I was the only one in the neighborhood who had one, so I felt extra special and even more proud. Each afternoon after school, I rode my beautiful bike up and down the street, grinning and laughing all the way. My father was the one who bought the bike for me, and I loved it that much more because he did.

Growing up, I spent a lot of time with my father. I remember sitting on his leg, outside on the porch, listening to him tell stories. I also enjoyed riding in his T-Model Ford, which I fondly called "the tick-i-licker." The bond I shared with my father was unbreakable.

While my father took the responsibility of providing financially for the family, my mother took responsibility for our spiritual well-being. To ensure we were spiritually grounded, she took us to church on a regular basis, so we could develop a relationship with our heavenly father. We attended union meetings by way of the bus and Sunday worship service and Sunday school on a weekly basis.

At our church, we would often have revivals that would last for two weeks. I witnessed the power of God move in the place as miracles flowed throughout the building. People came in drunk but left out sober, and the sick were healed of various diseases. All of that took place in our little old-fashioned country church that was fully equipped with a heater in the back. Near the heater is where the women sat and fed their babies, keeping them comfortable and quiet, while Elder Wynn, our pastor, delivered the sermon. He was a dynamic speaker. As the miracles continued to move about, the members were slain in the spirit, and many spoke in tongues.

The revivals were not the only highlight of our church. For me, Sunday school was intriguing. I thoroughly enjoyed attending Sunday school with Mother Chapman. She taught me all about Jesus through a unique way of teaching Sunday school, which was with Sunday school cards instead of books like they use today. Each Sunday, the other children and I would go into our class, and Mother Chapman would give us a new Sunday school card. We were required to learn the Bible verse, so we could recite it the next Sunday.

Church was rather calm and attending on a weekly basis was a way of life for my siblings and me. However, as it has been said, "Expect the unexpected." At that time though, I did not know what was meant by the unexpected. But, soon I would quickly learn.

During one of the union meetings, when I was eight years old, a preacher spoke on the topic "Hell Fire." His message certainly grabbed and held my attention, to say the least. Right then and there, I decided hellfire was not something I wanted to ever endure. So at that moment, although I had been going to church for as long as I could remember, I decided to live for the Lord. After service, we went home, and I prepared for bed as usual. Not long after falling asleep, I had a nightmare that I still remember to this day. In the dream, flames leaped all around my body. I could literally feel the heat from them. The dream scared me to no end. It only confirmed the decision I had made just hours earlier: *Hellfire was not for me.*

By the time fifth grade rolled around, I was excelling in my studies, and I was even voted president of the student council. Not only was I academically inclined, but I also loved to engage in sports and other extracurricular activities. I played in tetherball tournaments, participated in talent shows, and learned to square dance. As a youth, I was a robust girl, but a few teachers made a few alterations to some items of clothing for me, so I could have suitable attire for the talent shows. They were a lot of fun, and I enjoyed them immensely.

During that time in my life (my elementary years), my relationship with my father was wonderful, and my interactions with my teachers and those in the community were favorable. However, I felt a change come about in the way my mother responded to me. She knew I loved my father unconditionally and that we had a bond that was unbreakable. However, there was a rift between my mother and father, and because of their disagreements, she didn't care for the affection I showed toward him. Her actions showed me on several occasions how dissatisfied she was with the love I openly displayed for my father.

Once when I was nine years old, I was playing with a neighborhood girl, and during the course of our playtime, the girl yelled out, "Audrey Pearl, you should not have done that!" Upon the girl's outburst, my mother came out, grabbed me by my hair, dragged me inside, and beat me, not bothering to ask what had occurred. To me, it seemed as though she took every opportunity she could to severely discipline me. Actually, she was taking the frustrations she had with my father out on me.

After some time, I grew very tired of the beatings, so one day, I opened the window and stuck my head out. My mother saw me and asked what I was doing, in a tone that demonstrated her disapproval. I replied, "Getting some air," as I inhaled and exhaled. For once, she ignored me and walked away.

By the time I had made it to the six grade, I was yet involved in community events and stage plays. At twelve years old, I was very aware of my surroundings, and I still believed I was living a good life. At the same time though, I started to reflect on my future and what types of occupations I would be able to engage in once I graduated high school. I had noticed the only occupations available in my town involved field work, and I knew that was definitely not for me.

Once I entered Thomas Jefferson Middle School, I really took an interest in history, which led me to reading a lot of history books and writing book reports. I continued along with my extracurricular activities and excelled in volleyball. I even enjoyed singing and even appeared on a television show to sing. However, I did not make the choir that year, and I was not involved in any talent shows.

As my mind both wandered and wondered, I once again took notice of the occupations that were available for me in my town and seriously considered how my life would be after high school and where I would live. I desired to have a career, and I wanted to see the world. But the question was, "How would I get out there to see it?" Eventually, I came up with the perfect answer. I was going to join the service, and inadvertently, I would see the world. Furthermore, I would have no children, and I would not marry. That became my decision and motivation for my future.

When I shared my brilliant idea with my mother, she looked at me and did not say a word. At that moment, I did not understand what her silence meant. I would later learn that she figured if I did not want to have children or get married and on top of it all join the service, I was probably a lesbian. So, she quickly devised other plans for me. It was always her desire for me to marry and have children.

To move her plan into motion, somewhere along the way, she chose Clarence, a friend of the family, to be my husband. He was seven years older than I was, and he was in the Navy. To ensure that Clarence and I would make a connection, she did not allow me to hang out or converse with other boys. However, when Clarence was home from the Navy, he was permitted to come to my house, and I could sit and speak with him and even go out on dates. He started to bring gifts for me when he would come by, which made my father furious, but he had lost his voice of authority in the house because of his extramarital activities. So, my fate was left in my mother's hands.

Not too long after I started dating Clarence, I became pregnant. There was a lot of talk throughout the town about my condition because I was a single young woman who would soon be a mother. Some were saying I was just a fast girl, while others were saying it was a case of statutory rape. To clear up the matter, my mother convinced a judge to allow Clarence and me to get married, but my father did not agree. He wanted me to give birth to the baby, then give the baby to my parents to raise, so I could continue with school. But that was not my mother's plan. She wanted me married, and that was the end of it. And, in an effort to continue to keep other guys away from me, she forced me to wear maternity clothes from the moment she learned I was pregnant even though I was not showing yet.

In June 1957, Clarence's father married us in his home. After the wedding, Clarence and I moved to San Francisco. At that moment, I reflected on my life and realized there I was pregnant and married, with no education. I felt completely in despair. And in the back of my mind, I remembered the dream of hellfire I had some years back. I wondered what would become of me.

Lessons Learned

At a young age, I learned very quickly that facts always override fantasy.

Therefore, I had to face the new responsibilities that had developed in my life.

As a result, I chose marriage versus being single and having a baby out of wedlock. For me, that was the best choice.

A Question to Ponder

Revisit your childhood momentarily, allowing your mind to recall times you spent with your family, at school, and during social, spiritual, and extracurricular activities. Which events helped to shape the person you are today? Which people greatly influenced your life- positively or negatively- and why? Were there any decisions made on your behalf with which you do/did not agree? What were they and how did they impact your life?

_____

_____

_____

_____

_____

_____

_____

_____

_____

_____

_____

_____

_____

_____

From the Valley to Victory!

Chapter Two

Marriage and Motherhood

After moving to San Francisco with my new husband, I lived with his sisters, who were absolutely wonderful and very thoughtful to allow me to live with them. During the time I spent with them (while my husband was away in the Navy), I learned so much about how to take care of myself and how to plan for my future. They taught me how to budget my money, and they also informed me that I needed to see a doctor during my pregnancy, for my wellbeing and my unborn child's wellbeing also. Being only fourteen at the time, I did not know nearly as much as they did or even how to go about the daily business of life. Up to that point, my parents had taken care of the household and all of my needs and had not taught me much about living life on my own.

When it was time to give birth to my first child, I delivered at Letterman Army Hospital in San Francisco. My husband was home for the weekend, so he was there for the birth of our son. Sometime later, at the age of fifteen, I left one sister-in-law's home to move in with another sister-in-law. During that time, I was pregnant with my second child, and I lived with her throughout my second pregnancy. Once again when it was time to deliver, I gave birth at Letterman Army Hospital. Thankfully though, Clarence just happened to be on leave when I gave birth. Leave allowed him to be able to witness the birth of our two children. For that, I was pleased.

When I turned sixteen, my two children and I were still living with my sister-in-law. But, her home was getting a little crowded for her family and mine. So one day, my sister-in-law took me to get an apartment. I was so very excited. Up to that point in my life, I had never lived on my own, without other adults (if I could be considered an adult). I was excited and looking forward to the new adventure, privacy, and real adulthood, although I was technically still a teenager.

When my husband came home to the apartment, I had furniture, a washing machine, and a dishwasher. The entire apartment was furnished and decorated in shades of pink and black. I had made an adorable home for my children and myself. To furnish the apartment, I had opened a Sears' account and purchased everything I needed. Furthermore, I had begun to receive my husband's government check, which was initially being sent to his mother's house. Asking her for our money was getting old, so I went over there and retrieved the check and began having the money sent directly to me. After all, I was his wife and I needed to provide for my children and myself, without having to ask another woman for an allowance of my husband's finances. That just did not make any sense to me.

To say the least, my husband wasn't very happy that I was on my own and doing well for myself. But what was I do to do when he was away on the USS Picket (a submarine)? He would be gone for thirty days at a time and would come home for only six days. So, essentially, I had to fend for myself and make sure our children were taken care of- without having a go between.

Other times when he was home on leave, he spent his days and nights drinking, as many sailors and other service personnel did. His drinking was nerve wracking. Due to his emotional and physical unavailability, I did not have anything to turn to for comfort. At that time, I was not attending church as much as I used to, and from time to time, I would go to the Kingdom Hall with my sisters who were Jehovah's witnesses. But, that did not do much for my nerves.

After a few months, my husband's drinking problem accelerated to the point where he would pawn items from our home to get the alcohol he wanted to consume. My marriage began to unravel right before my eyes. The pattern of drinking and constantly arguing about money continued until my husband was discharged from the Navy. Afterward, he was hired as a janitor; however, his need and desire to drink superseded the need he had to take care of his family. So, once again, I had to bear the burden of that load alone, even with him being physically present. As I witnessed the change in his attitude and behaviors, I became bitter, and subsequently, the marriage continued to unravel. It was going in a downward spiral from which there would be no return.

To add to my discontentment, my husband began hanging out at my aunt's house, which was nothing but a free-for-all. Anything and everything went on in that house, and Clarence was happy to be a part of it. He would be over there all day and all night. What he did not know was my younger cousins would keep me abreast of his activities while he was there in their home. They were the ones who informed me that he would be over there with other women. Once I received the message, I went over there to see for myself. And sure enough, there he was acting as though he did not have a wife and children at home. To say the least, I became unglued (to put it nicely). Maybe he did not know that I was not the one to play with.

Meanwhile, our money problems became exacerbated. So to stretch the money I had, I would shop at the cannery where the canned goods were much cheaper, mostly because many of the cans were dented and not suitable for normal store sales. To add to our troubles, he was constantly giving his money to his mother and one of his sisters. To compound my discontent, he would speak about his mother all the time saying how she would do this and how she would do that. Finally, I had had enough, and I asked him, "Well, why don't you go stay with her?" But instead of him leaving, I decided to leave.

I quickly learned, after three years of marriage, the relationship was no match for me. So, I packed up my children and moved back home as I felt that was my only choice other than staying with him.

And there was no way I was going to do that. Upon my departure, I had no expectations. All I knew was that at sixteen years of age, my dreams were shattered, and I needed new direction.

When I arrived to my parents' house, I knew in my heart that I would not be there long. And although my mother and I had developed a cordial relationship, I only stayed there two weeks. It was time for me to move on and begin a new chapter of my life.

Lesson Learned

As a child, I developed a concept of marriage by watching my parents. However, to my chagrin, I quickly learned my marriage was quite different from that of my parents.

In my situation, I was usually alone with my children (not counting my sisters-in-law or my nieces and nephews) because my husband Clarence was always away on a naval ship for thirty days and only home for six days at a time.

Furthermore, when he was home, he would rather drink instead of sitting down and having dinner with the family. Our ideas of family life most certainly clashed with one another. Therefore, it was up to me to set the pattern of home and family life that I desired for my children and myself.

A Question to Ponder

Having you ever experienced an abrupt change in your life that was completely unexpected? Share your experience here and the impact it had on you later in life. If the experience was a recent one, share how you currently feel about it and the possible impact it may have.

_____

_____

_____

_____

_____

_____

_____

_____

_____

_____

_____

_____

_____

_____

_____

Chapter Three

Single

In May 1960, I left my parents' home for the second and final time. I moved to Los Angeles with my older sister Frieda and her five children. Frieda was not a wealthy person by any means, and she took care of her five children with very menial substances. Because I was unemployed, she took care of my two children and me as well. I was very grateful to my sister for her hospitality, and to help do my part and to decrease the load on Frieda, I did much of the housework and cooking. Our seven children never knew times were hard because they always had food in their mouths, clothes on their backs, and a warm place to sleep. The nine of us made the best of our living situation.

About a year later, after I had begun to receive government assistance, I was able to move out of Frieda's home and into a studio house on 77th St. and Hoover. To make the money I was receiving monthly stretch and every dollar count, I used the budgeting and shopping skills my sisters-in-law had taught me a few years before. I shopped very thriftily, so the food and clothes I purchased would last. Despite our low-income lifestyle, my children were always clean and lived a very normal childhood.

Being a single parent involved many challenges and eye awakening experiences, such as keeping my children protected from adult affairs/business, making choices that were based on their well-being, and keeping them as my first priority.

As my family of three continued to thrive, we eventually moved out of the studio house and into a one-bedroom apartment on 77th St. and Figueroa, not far from where we were currently living. I soon learned that not only did I have to make decisions involving my children as a single woman, but I also had to make some decisions involving dating, being fully aware that my choices would impact my life as well as my children's lives.

As time went on, I met and started dating Preston. And, not long after, I learned I was once again with child. All I could do was shake my head and say, "Oh, Lord. I'm going down the tubes for sure now." Then, to my disappointment, Preston and I broke up. Therefore, I had to navigate through the pregnancy alone. By that time, I was nineteen years old with two children and one on the way.

After I gave birth, Preston finally made his way over to my home to see the baby. Being in his presence, during his visit, I knew that our relationship had changed. The closeness we once shared was no longer there, and we would not be getting back together or resuming our dating relationship. Not only that, but he chose not to help out with the baby- financially, emotionally, or physically. That made me extremely angry, and a violent argument ensued, which eventually led to a physical altercation.

After that night, I became isolated and wondered how I ended up in that position: single, with no relationship, and three children. *What would become of us?* I wondered.

From time to time, I would read my Bible, but my study time and my alone time with the Lord was not as it had been. Somehow and at some time, I had drifted away from Him.

Meditating on my circumstances, I would constantly say to myself, "There has to be a better way to live." I didn't know what it was or how to achieve it, so mostly I would find myself stunned by my reality and felt as though I had no way out. Nevertheless, I maintained and lived life one day at a time, which was sometimes problematic because I was hitting and missing with church, trying to stay afloat with raising my children.

Instead of attending worship services on a regular basis, I was learning about and engaging in different settings in the world, such as parties, card games, and get-togethers. But, in all I engaged in, I never dabbled in anything harmful, such as drugs. Of all that I experienced in the world, I never became attached to anything. Nothing satisfied me. I always felt a void- a longing for something deeper.

If I had a more stable spiritual life, things may have been different. One thing that for sure had not changed was the fear of death had not lifted from me. Through everything I had gone through since I was eight years old, I had never forgotten the feeling I had the night I had the 'hellfire nightmare.' And, it was just a matter of time before I learned just how much it would plague my life.

Lesson Learned

Living in the Los Angeles offered me the possibility of resuming my educational dreams that I had placed on hold.

Although I partook in the party life from time to time and failed to attend worship services on a regular basis, I quickly learned a worldly life was not the lifestyle for me. God was tugging at my heart, and I knew it. It would be just a matter of time before I surrendered.

A Question to Ponder

Describe a time that you longed for something that seemed to out of reach. What, if anything, did you do to try to attain it? Were you successful in your attempts? Why or why not? How did you feel afterward?

From the Valley to Victory!

Chapter Four
Regrouping

At the tender age of nineteen, I met someone with whom I became very smitten. I was tired of meeting guys who could not communicate effectively and had nothing to show or offer. That man, however, was different; his words and his fancy 1962 Chevy Impala made an impression upon me. Our unconventional meeting took place on Main Street, when he stopped traffic to take a close look at me. My sisters and I were walking down the street, heading to a nightclub one Saturday evening, after securing a babysitter for the night. I was only going because it was the thing to do. Truthfully, there was nothing that intrigued me about hanging out in a nightclub. At that time, the horrific dream that I had years before, my thoughts of education, and my desires for travel were all I ever really thought about. But, there we were, and there he was- standing outside his car talking to me- in the middle of the street.

As the man stood in the street trying to get my attention with a car full of his male friends, he asked where I was going. Once I informed him, he requested permission to take me to my destination. I refused his invitation and instead said, "No, meet me there and have the table set." He nodded, demonstrating he understood my request.

That night, we formally introduced ourselves, as Audrey and Herman. We danced and hung out, enjoying each other's company. At the end of the night, we exchanged phone numbers, and of course, he wanted to drive me home. For the second time that day, I refused his invitation. Instead, I invited him to come over to my home on Sunday at noon.

When Sunday arrived, he was prompt, and I was impressed. Timeliness was important to me, and I found unpunctuality a turnoff. When I greeted him at the door, I was wearing an apron because I was preparing Sunday dinner. My two oldest children were playing outside in the yard, and the baby was inside with me. I introduced him to the children and showed him my baby girl, who was six weeks at the time. When he saw the baby, his eyes glazed over, and he grabbed her, causing the receiving blanket that was wrapped around her to fall to the floor. He ran outside with the baby, jumped into his car, and started the engine. I did not know what to make of his behavior, so without even thinking too much about it, I followed quickly behind him and jumped into the passenger seat of the car.

Still looking mesmerized by the baby, he started to drive down the street while holding the baby in his left arm and driving with his right hand. The baby's hand touched the steering wheel also, and he took that as a sign that she could drive. Over and over he said, "She can drive." I screamed out in horror, "No, she can't!" Ignoring my outburst and still believing that the baby could drive, he slowed the car down, so the baby could steer the car on her own. I could not believe that he actually thought a six-week-old baby had the mental capacity and small motor skills to drive a vehicle. I continued to scream, "She cannot drive!" I had hoped he would stop the car.

Finally, seeing he was not coming to his senses on his own, I told him to turn the car around and to take us back to the house. After returning home, I instructed him to keep the receiving blanket on her. From what I was witnessing, he did not have much, if any, experience with babies or young children.

While I finished preparing dinner, he held the baby, cuddled her, and kissed her. Later, we enjoyed dinner with the children, and after they went to bed, we continued good conversation, made promises to one another, and essentially our relationship started.

Along the way though, I learned he was a ladies' man and there were some issues that needed to be resolved before we could date freely. Moving forward, it took approximately six months for those personal issues to be resolved, and I'm not sure all of them were actually resolved during that time although he assured me they had been.

When the time came for him to meet my family, they were not impressed with him or fond of him in the least. Regardless of their lack of interest in him, I was very much interested. As a result, I was willing to live in his world rather than live without him in mine, as the famous Gladys Knight said in one of her songs.

As time went on, our relationship developed through the everyday ups and downs, the good times and the bad. Before long, I found myself with child again at twenty years old. Although the child would be my fourth, it would be his first even though he was seventeen years older than I was. (That explained his inexperience with children.)

I was conflicted about having another baby. On one hand, I knew he was a good catch, for he was a hard-working man for the state of California. He worked in a warehouse, and at that time, he was driving a 1965 Chevy Impala. (He had upgraded.) On the other hand, we weren't married. To make matters worse, my family was upset about me being pregnant again, which only led to quarrels. Then, he and I began to quarrel, and it did not appear that the relationship was going anywhere. I started having thoughts that once again I would be stuck on my own with another baby.

Disappointed by my newfound revelation, I ended the relationship, not waiting for nature to take its course. I figured if I was going to be on my own that I might as well start right then. For the next six months, as I went through the final two trimesters of the pregnancy, Herman and I did not see each other. I was so very disappointed that my heart became hardened, and I became bitter about relationships in general, my lack of education, and my inability to travel. I felt as though my life was going nowhere. Make no mistake about it- I loved my children, but I had thought my life was going to go down a different course. Boy, was I mistaken!

The baby was born on July 2, 1965. Four days later, on July 6, Herman came to see the baby for the first time. When he walked through the door, I was breastfeeding. He was so amazed by the activity that he just stood and stared. Finally to eliminate the awkwardness, I told him to have a seat. He complied.

After the baby was fed, I asked him if he wanted to hold his son. He said, "Yes." But then he said, "No, I can't." I took that to mean he didn't quite know how to handle a newborn. So, I put the baby on a pillow, so he would be able to hold him with ease. As he was holding our son, my daughter was standing right next to him. She had not seen him for six months and had obviously missed him. He was really the only father she had known. He hugged her, demonstrating that he had missed her as well. After two hours of visiting with us, he left, but he said he would be back. That visit rekindled our relationship, and I felt joy return to my heart.

After spending a little time with him, I quickly learned there were factors in his life that had not changed: He was still a ladies' man. As a result, the relationship I desired to have with him was not in view. And although I had feelings for him, my attention was turned toward God. I knew if I didn't make it to church soon, I would not last. A fear began to develop in me that doom was in my near future if I did not straighten my life out. Furthermore, I was fearful that the dream of hellfire would manifest in my life. The fear was so strong that I was not able to fully interact or converse with Herman.

Then, to make matters worse, on one occasion, a man broke into my home, and I took that as a clear sign that my life was in danger. I became so fearful of dying, and I truly believed I would not live to make it to the end of the year. To exacerbate my belief and my fear, every time I saw a station wagon going down the street, it looked like a hearse. That scared me even more, elevating my sense of trepidation. To add to my concerns, marriage was not in sight. So, in sin I remained.

One night, when I was twenty-one years old, I had a conversation with God, asking Him if He would allow me to live until that Sunday. I promised if I lived, I would go to church. When Sunday arrived, I was still alive. So, as I had promised, I went to church. Mother Hale, the supervisor of women, was preaching that night. As I listened to her sermon, I was like a bird with its mouth open, ready to receive nourishment. When I departed church that evening, I felt so much better, while at the same time having mixed emotions about my relationship. I, at that point, was fully aware that the relationship had to be dissolved, or we needed to get married, for I wanted to be in God's will. I refused to live a life of sin any longer.

The next time Herman came to my home, I explained the situation to him, and he unequivocally stated he did not want to dissolve the relationship. But from that point forward, our relationship was not the same, and eventually, it came to an end. However, he continued to fulfill his family responsibilities by taking care of our son, picking him up to go various places, and making sure my little girl was cared for. That pattern continued for two or three years. Although our feelings had not dissipated, we did not have an intimate relationship nor did we act on our feelings.

One day, he came by my house to take me shopping for our son, and along the journey, we ended up in a compromising position that I really did not want to be in. I told him I was saved, and I wanted to live a life that was pleasing to God. In so many words, he basically said he did not care. He wanted what he wanted at that moment. That compromising position led to baby number five.

Realizing I was pregnant, my world was turned upside down. There I was going to prayer every day and working in the church and ended up pregnant – again! I asked myself how I was going to reconcile my behavior with God. The only thing I could come up with was to leave the church, for I had messed up. So, that is what I did. And, ironically, no one in the church contacted me after I had left. And although I had made the choice to leave the church, I did not give the option of leaving to Herman. I told him in no uncertain terms he would not be leaving me, but instead he would be marrying me. So, he moved into my home with my children and me. He hesitated a little along the way, but I convinced him with my combative behavior. Despite his uncertainties about getting married, he was excited to have a second child. That time, he was there for the delivery and the raising of his second son. After that, he never left again.

The baby was born in 1969, and finally in 1971, we decided to join together in holy matrimony after straightening everything out in our lives. Our children were the ring bearers and the flower girls. One of my childhood friends was my matron of honor, and her boyfriend was the best man. We had a simple chapel wedding followed by a very large reception. My father and other family members attended the wedding.

Before the evening ended, my father said down with me, and we had a cup of coffee. He wanted to share a bit of advice with me about what was about to take place in my life. Because he was my father, I took his words to heart. He said, "If you need me, call. Herman is a good man. He will take care of you and these children. And I can't say nothing else." I knew precisely what those words meant. That was his simple way of warning me that once a ladies' man always a ladies' man.

Herman had been in my life since 1962. From the moment, I knew my life would be fine. Actually, it would be better because he was an excellent provider. However, there was emptiness in my heart due to not attending church. That was something I would definitely need to reconcile- soon.

As far as I was concerned, my life had taken a turn for the better- financially speaking. I had the privilege of being able to buy what I wanted. I was able to attend church events and other special events without a problem although I didn't go on a regular basis.

Then, God called me to ministry, and I could not ignore the call. Meanwhile, our marriage was rocky due to my husband's philandering. Nevertheless, God's call resounded in my ear. Then, I decided returning to God was my only option. So, I, at that point, restarted my Christian journey- after having committed the cardinal sin. I had to return to the roots of holiness because they were weighing heavily on my heart. I knew full well that my marriage was not the will of God for me. But, I made every attempt to make it work with all my being.

Lessons Learned

I learned to never allow the lust of the eye to be the compass of my life. Although something may look appealing from the first glance or even after a long stare, it does not mean accepting it into your life is the best choice.

Additionally, I learned finances can bring happiness, but that state is only temporary. It is joy that is long lasting.

A Question to Ponder

Have you ever been faced with having to choose the lesser of two evils? Describe the situation, fully detailing the two choices. Then, explain your choice. What specifically assisted you in making your choice? What was the outcome?

From the Valley to Victory!

Chapter Five
Family Life

From Saturday to Thursday, Herman was a family man. He worked every day and had dinner with the kids and me at 5 PM daily. Before dinner, he even prayed, as he had a foundation in the church from when he was a youth. Furthermore, each of the children said a verse before dinner. From time to time, Herman would attend church services with us, but of course, he was not as dedicated or involved as I was. I belonged to several auxiliaries, and after recommitting my life to Christ and rejoining the church, there were considerable differences within the church as it related to people's attitude towards me.

Before my marriage, most of the people were standoffish because I was a single mother with several children from different fathers. However after I married, I became respectable in their eyes. Generally speaking, people were nicer to me and my children. Prior to my marriage to Herman, my children were never invited to sleep over the other children's houses, and I had a difficult time getting a ride to and from church, when I did not drive Herman's car.

Here are some examples to demonstrate how my children and I were treated prior to my marriage to Herman. On one occasion, I had solicited a ride after Sunday worship service and my children and I were about to enter the woman's vehicle. She stopped abruptly and told me to clean my baby's hands before he got in the car. She said it as though he had bubonic plague. I was utterly offended, so I walked home.

On another occasion, after service one day, a funeral for a church member was being held. Wanting to attend, I volunteered to go with a group of women to the funeral. They said, "You need to ask the pastor for permission." I did not understand why I needed permission to pay my last respects, but I did as they had suggested. When I approached the pastor, he said, "Sis. Audrey, well you know how people are." I responded, "Do you mean to tell me you don't want me to go to the funeral with you." They just stammered. Not wanting to engage any longer, I said, "That's okay." I left and walked home, not even bothering to ask anyone for a ride.

On Wednesday nights, our church was usually filled with people. One particular Wednesday, my sister went up to teach and during her message, she said, "Sis. Lewis (referring to me) is alright, but she likes her beer and her boyfriend."

My sister was not the only one who made comments about me over the pulpit, for the entire congregation to hear. One of the mothers said my daughters' dresses were nice but cheap. That stung! Later, after marriage, I brought it up to the offender by asking, "Are my daughters' dresses cheap now?" reminding her of what she had said. You see, after I was married, I had more money at my disposal, and I was able to spend a little more money on quality items although there was nothing wrong with my children's clothing before.

Those comments, others like it, and people's negative attitude toward me was not only hurtful, but discouraging as well. I had been labeled from the beginning. One reason is because I would speak my mind, in addition to the second reason of being a divorcee with young children and having others out of wedlock.

What most people were unaware of was I had the gift of discernment, but I did not know I had it, so I did not know to use it discretely. Things would be going on, and I would open my mouth and speak out of turn about what I discerned in the spirit. People would be offended, but they would later find out that what I said was true. The gift I had showed me more than I wanted to know. One lady told me, "The gift you have probably keeps you miserable because you see so much." She was right.

One day, while wearing light makeup and a dress that was slightly above my knee, I was told to my face that I looked like a whore. People's ignorance kept them from seeing my efforts to live a holy life. There I was giving God all I had- in the face of adversity. It was that kind of treatment and unacceptance that made me move forward with Herman. I figured they weren't happy about anything I did, so what difference did it make whom I married.

To make matters worse, the rude and belittling comments I suffered through were not only directed towards me, but people had the audacity to tease one of my sons because of his size. In his defense, I said, "He is smart."

Furthermore, the church folk had an issue with giving credit to whom credit is due and with only having specific people involved in services. On Women's Day, I was never asked to do anything, and when I inquired about serving and being involved, I was told, "We don't know about you."

From the Valley to Victory!

I was so hurt and offended that on another occasion when the pastor asked who was going to heaven, I said, "No, not if you all are going to be there."

Then, an opportunity came for me to put a service together. So, I held a candlelight service. It was very beautifully decorated, and I spent my own money to do so. After the service, the pastor got up there and gave the credit to me *and* his wife who had nothing to do with it whatsoever.

After I was married, I was asked to moderate, but the pastor's wife did not want me to do so. I called her and asked why she was against me moderating. She did not give me a straight answer. *In my disappointment*, I had a few choice words with her. Later, the pastor came to me and said, "Audrey, my wife told me what you said to her." I said, "Yes and I told my husband what she said to me." He had no more to say on the matter.

On another occasion, I was invited to be on a program and was asked what I wanted to do for the service. I said, "I'm going to be dressed." My sassy comment was ignored, and the question, "What do you want to do?" came forth again. I said, "I just told you. I'm going to be dressed." Still ignoring my flippant attitude, it was said, "We need you to do something." Finally, I said in agreement, "Okay, I'll pray." But as I had forewarned, on the night of the program, I was fashionably dressed, and they probably couldn't focus on the prayer. By that time, I had just had it with them, and I wanted them to know exactly how I felt.

When I was pregnant with my last baby (prior to getting married), someone had suggested giving me a baby shower. Pastor said, "No, we don't do that for unmarried people." "But it may encourage her," the person suggested, as she knew what had been happening to me and could sense my discouragement. The pastor did not budge on his stance.

Later, the time for revival had come, and I had to organize it. I was told that someone else would run it in my place with the excuse that the person had never seen me run a revival. He said, "I hope you understand." I said, "I hope you do too." I did not attend the revival, and consequently, I left the church. My reputation followed me to another church. Sometimes, I was so distraught I just stayed home.

During my disconnection with the church, God spoke to me and said, "You threw away everything I gave you- offices and positions." I admitted my shortcomings saying, "Yes, I did." I was hurt. I permitted church hurt to prevent me from walking in my God-ordained calling. And, to top it off, a lot of what was being said was lies.

For example, at one time, a pastor called me and claimed I had been talking about him and one of the sisters and said I had better get it straight that very day and hung up in my face. Later, the pastor called and apologized, asking "You didn't do that did you?" I told him, "I said I did not when you asked me. I told you when I first came to this church that if I called saying I was in jail due to beating up husband, I did it. Anything else, I did not."

I really tried to avoid the type of treatment I suffered, but I had no control over what others said and did. In my disgust and grave disappointment in the behavior of the 'saints,' I told God if He ever gave me a position of authority, I would never treat His people that way. Instead, I would be encouraging.

Still dealing with various levels of ignorance and jealousy, one day, I decided I needed a more reliable vehicle, so I went out and purchased a BMW. When I pulled into the church parking lot, the pastor was standing outside. When he saw me, he said, "I didn't know you were buying that." I said, "I didn't know I had to tell you." After getting out of the car, I walked inside. Later in the service, when offering time came around, the congregation was asked for a $5 offering. I only had a $50 bill. They tried to take $10, but I told them no- adamantly. They were not going to take my money. We actually had a verbal altercation right there at the offering table, until the pastor chimed in and asked if there was an issue. I quickly responded, "No," while giving the deacon the evil eye and telling him to give me the correct change.

Most of the negativity occurred prior to me being married. After the marriage, however, my children were treated as any other child was treated, and we never had a problem getting a ride to and from church if Herman's car was unavailable to me. Thankfully, Herman did not have a problem with me going to church or attending prayer meetings on Wednesday and Sunday. While there, I assisted the Dr. Shumate.

Dr. Shumate taught us door-to-door witnessing. He also taught me how to run revivals and showed me how the Spirit of God moves, how not to be rigid, and how to get out of the box when ministering. At that time, the State Elect Lady was Mother Rebecca Smith. I served under her, and as the youngest woman, I was the gopher (the 'go for'), meaning I had to run the errands. I had to 'go for this' and 'go for that.'

Dr. Shumate and Mother Smith emphasized that souls must be reached at any cost. Prayer was the first dynamic of evangelism, followed by bringing the souls in, then feeding the natural man, being hospitable, and then finally meeting the needs of the whole man.

In the ministry, altar workers were selected, as it was an elite position. As an altar worker, if someone fell under the anointing of the Holy Spirit, the altar worker was required to kneel and pray until something happened. When Mother Morris, who was the State Supervisor, organized the third generation of COGIC missionaries, my name was added to the list. I considered it an honor. The purpose of the group was to demonstrate the ongoing instilment of COGIC in children. We had to be ready at all times to speak, be prepared for convocation on Women's Day, at women's convention, and our workers' meetings. That was an extremely exciting time for me.

Soon after, Elder Shumate was appointed National Regional President of the Evangelist Department. And, I was appointed

National Regional Hospitality President of the National Regional Evangelist Department. Although I had a new position, I was still operating in the capacity of gopher. My duties as the Regional Hospitality President were to prepare meals for women's day and men's day and to have snacks available for visiting ministers. At times, I would take a portion of my grocery money to prepare the meals at church, so the church would not be required to bear the burden.

During that time, I found myself at ease and feeling rewarded by working in God's vineyard. My children stayed home with my husband, and when I wanted to attend a special church engagement, I would be back at home each night to have his favorite dinner and pie waiting for him. While he would be in the midst of eating his meal, I would say, "There's a meeting at church, and I would like to go," and he would be very agreeable.

Meanwhile, to strengthen our family relationship, every year, we drove to Madera on Memorial Day to be with my father. Also, my husband and my father would take fishing trips together, thereby strengthening their bond. On various occasions, we would drive up to the Salton Sea to camp and fish. Herman loved being a family man so much that he would spontaneously host barbecues and invited family and friends over, just so we could all be together and have a good time. And it did not have to be a special day or holiday.

Sunday, however, was considered as a special day. We deemed it to be family day. We had prayer and talked about what was going on in everyone's life. Also every day as we sat around the dinner table, each child had an opportunity to share how his or her day was at school, what he or she enjoyed, and any problems he or she may have had.

Each Labor Day, the entire family would drive up to Orville, California to see my brother and his wife. While we were there, my oldest two children would visit with their dad Clarence, after visiting with my father. Clarence never really had a relationship with his children outside of the times they would inadvertently go to his house to spend the night only because they were in near proximity to his home by being at their grandfather's house.

So that was family life with my husband and I and our five children. Because the older two had a father with whom they were in contact, Herman did not feel it was his place to overstep boundaries and impede upon their father's territory. So, he had a respectful and loving relationship with my two children, while he specifically "fathered" the youngest three. Being mindful that they were all children, he was careful to treat all of them the same.

Despite the loving moments our family shared from Saturday to Thursday, every Friday night Herman would go out, stay out all night, and not return until Saturday. Ironically, he never engaged in that type of particular behavior while we were living together; he only engaged in it once we were married. Why the change? To this day, I do not know.

Once I realized my husband's extramarital behaviors would continue, I began to complain about not having a car. From the time Herman left home to the time he returned again, the children and I would be without transportation. Therefore, we would be unable to take care of any errands or any activities in which we wanted to engage. So, I began to complain and complain until Herman purchased a car for me, which was a Ford Pinto. In my new automobile, I was able to visit my dad and run errands.

Then, a change came about. At the age of thirteen years old, my oldest son became too much to handle, so I sent him to live with his father because he continuously indulged in disobedient behavior. I would not tolerate disobedience in my home, so it was best for him to leave. Once he left, he never returned to my home to live on a permanent basis. At that time, we lived in a five-bedroom house. The children had Ping-Pong tables and games with which to play. They had a very comfortable life.

However, in 1973, as my children were growing up, my oldest daughter began to have social difficulties, so we moved into a three-bedroom house in a gated community. At that time, I was well cared for and living in a new community with my four children and husband. Life was good.

However, I began to have a desire to continue my education again. Consequently, I enrolled in Compton High Adult School to earn my high school diploma. That did not work out the way I planned, but I did get an opportunity to do arts and crafts at home and learn to cook different foods from cookbooks. One of the things I learned how to make was caramel candy. Afterwards, I decided to take a cooking class at Compton College. I was there for one whole semester when my husband decided he didn't want me to be away from home so much, as I was gone for both school and church on a regular basis. My desire for God was stronger than my educational desires although me desire for education was a burning desire. So, I decided to discontinue school at that time.

From the Valley to Victory!

Lesson Learned

My education was placed on hold, so I could attend to what was most important to me: God, my husband, and my children.

The Word of God says, *"But seek ye first the kingdom of God, and his righteousness; and all these things shall be added unto you"* (Matthew 6:33, KJV). And for me, God would soon deliver on His word!

A Question to Ponder

Sometimes in life, we may feel unfairly marginalized (kept out of mainstream events) or ridiculed. Has there ever been a time when you felt that way? If so, when? What did you do? What advice would you give to someone who found him/herself in that position?

Chapter Six
Church

In 1973, as I continued to work with the Evangelist Department, at the local, state, and regional levels, I took a job at the Orthopedic Hospital, working in surgery, in the instrument room as a technician. They offered on-the-job training, so I was able to learn everything I needed to know to do my job well. At that time, my youngest was in nursery school, so I did not have to be concerned about a babysitter or being home myself. The position was short lived; it lasted for only six years.

At that same time, Elder Shumate had witnessed my works for the Lord (being diligent for God) and considered me as a candidate for state licensure. As a result, I went before the board and received my license. The Evangelist Department had two boards: one for the men and one for the women. The women's board consisted of old mothers and some licensed evangelists, who were knowledgeable about the Bible and women's work in the church (at that time).

To be considered for work in the department, the board asked candidates questions, such as, "What does the Bible say about your hands?" (Whatever your hands find to do, do with all your might.) The board also asked mothers about their children, if they were young, as the children were their first responsibility. The board believed even if a woman were married, she should not leave the children too long with her husband. Those were the main questions that were asked, in addition to being required to know who the state supervisor, district missionary, your pastor, and your bishop are. The board didn't ask too much about anything else. And, if the questions were answered favorably, you were permitted to work in ministry.

When I went before the board and was asked about my children and their well-being, I answered, "I will work locally, in the district, and the state until my children leave home or go to college." I had really accepted the idea of working in the church and was very comfortable with it, regardless of what else was going on in my life.

During that same time frame, my second daughter was in Upward Bound. As a result, she was on college campuses getting her education, embracing her future career as a nurse. I had always pushed her to become self-sufficient, and she was working as a certified nursing assistant. With all that she had learned, she was a great help to me when I became ill. I had been suffering from a large oblong knot in the knee area of my right leg that was the size of a football. And, when I went to Texas for a family visit, I would fall as I was walking, not knowing what was ailing me.

My daughter looked at my knee, saw the knot, and said, "Mom, you have a tumor." I went to the hospital to have it diagnosed and ended up having surgery. As I lay at home recuperating, I finally determined that I had had enough of my life as it was. I said, "This is it!" At that moment, I declared I was going to get my education, and I did not care who did not want me gone from home. I also declared they could leave if they did not like it.

In 1981, I enrolled in Jordan Locke Adult School. I took classes for six months, took the GED test, passed it, and two months later found another school in Santa Monica and enrolled. My family life continued as normal, and I continued with my responsibilities of cooking and cleaning for my family. That summer, my husband took a vacation to Texas, and while he was away, I took the entrance exam for the LVN classes. As I waited for the exam results, I went shopping for two hours. Upon my return, I was informed that I had passed and was granted entrance. School was scheduled to begin in

December. To say I was extremely ecstatic and excited about my new venture would be an understatement.

Lessons Learned

I learned to be patient and to allow patience to have its perfect work (James 1:4). Doing so allowed an opportunity for the completion of my education to come to fruition.

A Question to Ponder

Have you ever experienced a burning desire to do something, but every time you reached toward the goal, it seemed to get further and further out of your grasp? Did you eventually conquer your desire? If so, how? If not, devise a plan that will allow you to see your desire fulfilled.

_____

_____

_____

_____

_____

_____

_____

_____

_____

_____

_____

_____

From the Valley to Victory!

Chapter 7
Disruption of Marriage

Upon my husband's return from Texas, he let me know under no uncertain terms would he support me going to school and that he would not tolerate it. He also informed me that if I could not obey, I had to leave the house and if I did choose to leave, our marriage was over. I said, "We've been through a long time ago, so I'm packing." He was shocked at my response, as he fully expected me to go along with his every word and desire. I left out happily, as I looked forward to move my educational plan into motion. I moved in with my oldest daughter, who had had a baby sometime prior and had left home and got her own apartment. I started school on the right track; I was getting good grades, and I was pleased. Meanwhile, I would hear from my kids often and see them on a weekly basis – in my new home with my daughter.

During the time I was in school, my church life diminished. I explained to Dr. Shumate about school, and he placed someone else as the Hospitality President, but he let me know to inform him when I wanted to return. He was a great proponent of education, so he understood completely. During that time, I only participated in leading devotional services and other minor activities, such as prayer. Additionally, I continued to attend meetings, when they were in Los Angeles.

1982 came in, and I found myself very happy, but I missed my children greatly. But I had peace in knowing that upon graduating, I could get them once I completed my ten-month program. However, the tables were turned. On March 10, 1982, I lost my second son. While I was at school, a phone call came in alerting the school that I needed to return home at once because my son had been shot. When I received the news, I said, "He's dead."

The Lord had showed me in a dream six weeks prior that something devastating was about to happen. In the dream, I was back in Compton, and Dr. Shumate and his wife were standing on the steps in dark clothing. I could sense the doom in the atmosphere. A conversation ensued, but when I awoke from the dream, I could not remember what had been said. I just knew the news they had come to deliver was unpleasant. So when I said my son was dead – he was. I later learned that an hour before he died, he had told his younger brother, "I feel like I'm going to be killed," as they sat eating macaroni and cheese. Obviously, his brother did not take him seriously because his only response was, "Well, give me your mac 'n cheese." Not too long afterward, my son was shot in the street.

The death of my son is what reunited my husband and me. Before the funeral took place, Herman said to me, "Come home. It's okay that you're going to school. Just come back." At that point, I had been gone for a total of six months. I complied and returned home.

For the funeral, Herman's family came in from Texas and mine came in from all over. When we reunited, we simply picked up from where we had left off. The Friday night escapades restarted a month later. I guess my husband had ceased his activity while I was gone because he needed to be home with our children. Determined, I continued to attend school and focused on my studies and not on my husband's activities. I could see the light at the end of the tunnel. Although I wanted my relationship to work with my husband, the factors remained the same, and I could no longer tolerate it.

On June 9, 1982 at 5:30 AM, as I was getting ready for class, the phone rang. I've learned that my oldest brother had passed. My youngest daughter and I were attending school together, so I told her to go ahead and go to class and inform the school of what had happened and that I would not be in that day because I needed to go to Orville. My husband took off from his job to go with me, and we were gone for five days. Once we had laid my brother to rest, I returned home and went back to school. After my brother's passing, everything returned to normal. I was even more determined to finish school, and I did just that.

Graduation was scheduled for September. However, my concentration was poor at times with all of that was a going on in my life. But thanks to God, I came out of class with a B average. Then, when I went before the state board, I passed the very first time.

Lesson Learned

One of my biggest life lessons was to persevere because perseverance brings dreams and aspirations into existence. Giving up prematurely will only lead to further disappointment.

God gives us the desires of our heart. My desire was to begin my career. I did so by finishing school and passing the board exams.

A Question to Ponder

How important has education, career, or traveling been to you?

On a scale of 1-10, how would you rate your desires and why?

From the Valley to Victory!

Chapter Eight
Actualization

I was finally able to pursue what I had started years prior as a child- my education. The nursing courses I had enrolled in were rather easy, due to the previous involvement I had in the medical field. Finding a position was just a matter of time. Working at Kaiser was a good time, and there were many options available. They had plenty of opportunities to go to school two days a week and work three days a week to become an RN. They would pay for the classes as well. However, it was at that time that my home life became difficult. I felt as though I was midway up the hill in accomplishing my education, and nothing could stop me. Although the opportunity to work and go to school intrigued me, I put it on hold and pursued my present career to the full extent, by working for other agencies in the evening or on my days off. By doing so, I was able to explore other opportunities in my scope of practice.

As a LVN, my social life became more upscale as I engaged with doctors and nurses, but the lifestyle did not suit me. My heart and my soul longed for Christ. I returned to my spiritual desires while still embracing what I had learned in my career. My longing led me back to St. John with Dad Shumate, where I resumed my responsibilities as pastor's aide and in the Evangelist Women's Department. At that time, traveling with the church had become very prevalent. We traveled locally for different meetings and tent revivals that were held on E. 14th St. in Oakland. Our regular meetings were held in Arizona, Nevada, Utah, New Mexico, and both Northern and Southern California. At that point, I was no longer the gopher. Rather, I was in the heart of the meetings, as I functioned as an official. My heart, my spirit, and my soul were happy because evangelism was my passion!

Lessons Learned

God's call is the highest call in the land. The work of God is the most satisfying in the world!

God's work brings everlasting life, hope, and healing, in self, families, and marriage/relationships!

From the Valley to Victory!

A Question to Ponder

There is always a season to rejoice! Can you recall a time in your life where you felt everything was just perfect because all your dreams and desires had been fulfilled? Share your experience below.

_____

_____

_____

_____

_____

_____

_____

_____

_____

_____

_____

_____

_____

_____

Chapter Nine
Social Life

My marriage was on the brink of utterly failing. Our finances had declined, and our relationship was not thriving. One day, I told Herman if I ever learned that we were never married, I would leave. From an unction in my spirit, I called downtown and learned that the papers for his divorce were never finalized. Thus, he was still legally married to his last wife and not me. All the things that had transpired throughout the years, I had accepted to a degree, but that was one thing I would not accept because it would interfere and possibly cost me my soul. Having reviewed every avenue and every road and every part of my being, there was no way I would succumb to Herman's shenanigans.

It was a costly decision, but I had learned whatever God does not bless in the beginning, He would never bless. Therefore, the demise of my marriage had come to pass. But I picked up the pieces after learning my husband was a bigamist and after he told me, "No one will make me do something I don't want to do." That had been his response when I asked him to marry me legally after learning our marriage was not legal. Upon his refusal, I knew what I needed to do.

Four months later, I left my home and lived with my sister for a couple of weeks until I found a one-bedroom apartment to live in- with no husband and no children. When I had moved, I left everything behind, except for my microwave, VCR, and TV. I was very excited because that was the first time that I would live completely alone. I wasn't required to cook for anyone, bathe anyone, or lay out clothes for school.

As a newly single woman, my nursing friends cradled me back into the single life and gave me tips on how to live as a single woman, without offending other women who are married by asking their husband for assistance with things, such as my car. One friend in particular told me to go and get AAA, so I would always have assistance with my car with fixing flat tires, etc. She also recommended having a handyman to help around the house. My friends also advised me to find a good mechanic, but I had to ensure he understood that he would only maintain my car and nothing else. In our spare time, my friends and I went to birthday parties and BBQs.

Meanwhile, my career was flourishing, and I was then able to work more hours at night with the registry. It was at that point that I was trying to go back to college. I purchased an old car (another Pinto) that only went forty-five miles an hour, and I enrolled into Trade Tech. I wanted to stay abreast of what was going on in the world, so I took general education and psychology courses for about one year. Then, I revisited the option of becoming an RN. As I did so, I noticed that my church life was suffering once again, but I figured I'd pick it back up later.

I enrolled in Cerritos College because I wanted to take science classes, but I heard the Lord say "no" due to the type of person I was. I wanted to work for Him, but at the same time, I wanted to live lavishly. Being disobedient, I enrolled into a science class anyway. One night, I went to class, and it took me two hours to find my way back home. I was very scared of what that meant and what God was saying to me. So, I decided not to return to that class anymore. I did not even take the time to withdraw properly from the class. Essentially, God was saying my travels would take me away from Him, and He wanted my full attention as it related to serving Him. At that point, I made myself satisfied with my career as it was.

Later on, I did have the opportunity to travel. I went to the Bahamas with the church. I was very excited to see a new place. It was a new adventure for me. So much so that when I returned home, as I focused on furnishing my home, I began to look for the next place to travel. At that time, church was still a part of my life but not as it should have been. In 1988, my oldest son asked me to go to Evangelistic COGIC with him.

I decided to go and learned Elder Charles Lollis was the pastor. We had known each other from years before, and when he saw me, he asked, "Is that Audrey? Come down here. Let us see you." So, I promptly strutted down the aisle in my wrap dress, and he prayed for me saying, "Lord, you kept her." He grabbed me and repeated the same phrase again, as he looked at me as though he was looking deeply into my soul. The next Sunday, I went back to the church again, and I shouted and danced, but I did not join at that point.

Back at my church, I told my mother in the gospel (my older sister) that I was discontinuing my membership. She got very upset and felt as though I would not behave properly away from the fellowship (according to the Word of God). Sometimes, she was right. In her disappointment in me, she said a few harsh words that really stung.

From the Valley to Victory!

Going back to my son's church, I decided to join. Two months later, as we were walking out of service, the pastor stopped me and said, you can teach my prayer and Bible Band. I said, "Oh really?" Before I knew it, I was the teacher, and the Bible Band grew from 3 students to 90 in one month. The work I did in the ministry at that point was the same as the work I had done before. I worked at the local, state, and district levels. But then the devil turned his ugly head and jealousy came on the scene. People came from all around to join the class. As a result of the class' growth, the treasury also grew. With money, greed can often follow. In that case, it did. The money was taken from the treasury, and eventually, the class was shut down.

Soon after, the position for State Elect Lady became available, and God put it on Pastor Lollis' heart to appoint me for the position. After my appointment, the department grew by leaps and bounds. For our meetings, people would be standing outside to get in. Pastor Lollis had the gift of healing cancer, and I had the gift of laying on hands. When we were in revivals, they were packed out, and some people unfortunately were turned away. Souls were saved, healed, delivered, and set free. People who were blind left seeing.

The services were so anointed that the head the National Evangelist Department of COGIC heard about the meetings and the National President of the Evangelist Department came to witness the mighty move of God. In his presence, God did no less that time than He had done in any of the other meetings. The 'go ye' bus went to all churches in the jurisdiction that wanted us to come. Monthly newsletters were sent out detailing our events and activities, to keep everyone abreast of all that was going on. Evangelism was our passion and thrust, and we moved in the anointing of the Holy Ghost.

I was so excited about what God was doing that I would leave work at 7:30 AM to knock on doors and pass out tracks for upcoming revivals. And God did not disappoint. In the evenings, I would attend the state workers' meeting from 6 to 7 PM. I would attend the convocations and then our own meetings. The place was always packed.

Soon after, I became active once again with the National Regional Evangelists, as the State Elect Lady, with Dr. Shumate. With that change in my status, my duties also changed. I worked closely with the National Elect Lady during services and workshops. Through all that we did, God was always glorified. Furthermore, on men's day, which was similar to women's day, there were business meetings at both the state and regional level, and I attended when I could.

Meanwhile, continuing to be faithful to prayer and Bible band, I trained evangelists on how to run revivals. One night, during our revival, with the understanding that I cannot sing, I sang "I Don't Want Anyone's Blood on My Hands." A lady in the audience, who had obviously never heard the song, ran around the church yelling. She was very hard to calm down, but in the end, God truly blessed her.

Continuing to work in ministry, Pastor Lollis and I attended a state meeting in Pasadena, where I was the speaker, and the house was full. As I was speaking, a man entered, and I heard the Lord say, "Watch him." So, as I preached, I watched him. He approached me with his hands clenched into fists, and he had a look as if though he was going to hit me. I stopped preaching and began to sing, "Satan, the Lord Rebukes You." The man spun around to face the audience. He had no idea what had happened to him. A few men came and sat me down and prayed over me.

All in all, the life of evangelism was rewarding. Eventually, Elder Lollis was asked to be State President for another jurisdiction. He called me to work with him, and I responded, "Major things are happening now." He ignored me and said, "Come on." In obedience, I followed. We set up meetings, and they had the same effect and the same outcome as they had had before.

At that time though, I did not work as closely with the women's supervisor as I should have. But, my name was still ringing in the National Department, so I was called to go to Memphis. After attending the meeting there, I didn't feel as though I could thrive at the National Level, so I opted to stay with the Regional Level. That lasted for approximately a year and a half, and then I decided to let some responsibilities go.

Eventually, I left Lollis' church, resigning from all positions. Later, I joined a church in Long Beach. Controversy overwhelmed me after being given a position. At that time, one of my sisters had passed on. Also, I had become slightly ill. Church responsibility was just too much to handle at that time.

Facing life, the disappointments, the complications of trying to live, I felt I needed to think and receive direction from the Lord. Meanwhile, I traveled quite a bit with people from the Evangelist Department and spoke out of the country, but I knew I needed divine direction. I had promised God when He healed my son, I would live for Him. I promised Him if He healed my baby, I would live for Him. On another occasion, I said if He would let me live until that Sunday, I would live for Him. Then, I had promised God if He would send me to a church where I felt loved and involved, I would give Him all I had to give. At that point, He led me to Love, Peace, and Happiness Family Christian Fellowship Church. He tugged on my heart about different things that were my fault. I repented, as I wanted to make the coast clear. So when I went to the new church, it was just a matter of when I was going to join.

From time to time, I survey the changes that have taken place over time. I look at the way ministry was conducted back when I was heavily involved and the way it is now. Today, ministers do not take the time with souls as we did back then. But God is yet saving daily as should be saved.

I am no longer a foot soldier, but I do pass out tracks at the market, and when people talk to me, I do all I can to introduce them to the Lord or at least invite them to a service. Also, God has once again called me into ministry, and in obedience, I answered His call. At Love, Peace, and Happiness Family Christian Fellowship Church, I serve as the president of the Redeemed Women's auxiliary, as the supervisor of women.

Lessons Learned

As Dad Shumate always said, "Audrey, God is faithful!" I have found on several occasions that his words were so true. God is faithful and He wants us to be faithful as well. *"Moreover it is required in stewards, that a man be found faithful"* (I Corinthians 4:2).

God did not want me involved in church scandal. He desired me to work in the vineyard without murmuring and complaining.

His word rings true in my life- *"Wherefore take unto you the whole armour of God, that ye may be able to withstand in the evil day, and **having done all, to stand***" Ephesians 6:13.

A Question to Ponder

Have you ever found yourself faced with a problem and you neglected to pray right away? Do you think if you had prayed earlier, you would have found your way sooner? Why or why not?

_____

_____

_____

_____

_____

_____

_____

_____

_____

_____

_____

_____

_____

From the Valley to Victory!

Chapter Ten
Submission

Jeremiah 31:3 says, *"The LORD hath appeared of old unto me, saying, Yea, I have loved thee with an everlasting love: therefore with lovingkindness have I drawn thee."*

When I first went to Love, Peace, and Happiness Family Christian Fellowship Church, I felt something I had never experienced in any church I had ever joined. It was the one element that I needed that had been missing for so many years before: the love of the saints of God. At LPH, the love enveloped me. And even though I felt and knew in my heart that the people loved me, I remained in a stand-offish condition. It was just my nature, after all the church hurt I had suffered. Even after a lovely young woman gave me a Valentine's Day gift and said, "I love you," (and still tolerates me to this day), it took me a while to warm up to the embraces and smiles that I received.

In that church, my presence and my input are valued. I found myself wanting to know more about God's Word, as theology is of great importance in that ministry. With a continued desire and longing for God's Word, I began to yearn for a biblical degree, so I needed to find a school that would serve my needs. As I delved into my studies, attended prayer meetings, and fulfilled speaking engagements, the love continued to surround me.

Jesus said, *"A new commandment I give unto you, That ye love one another; as I have loved you, that ye also love one another"* (John 13:34). The members of Love, Peace, and Happiness have abided by this commandment. And because of their love, I began to search the scriptures more and more, as a yearning and desire for God's truth burned deeply inside of me like never before.

Bishop Martin taught on how to deal with the aspects of everyday life, and he instructed us to read the book of Proverbs every day, saying it would show us how to live life. Following his guidance, I did as he had instructed. Doing so led me to rededicate, resubmit, and repent (realizing my flaws and taking responsibility for some of the things that had occurred in my life).

My rejoicing did not end there. One day, while Bishop was preaching, he read Job 36:11, *"If they obey and serve him, they shall spend their days in prosperity, and their years in pleasures."* From that day, submitting to the will of God became my focus. Loving my neighbor became a breeze for me; whereas, it had been difficult before. Furthermore, I stopped fighting God and accepted His will for whatever He had for me to do. At that point, I was willing to pick up my cross and follow Him daily. My faith was increased, and I read His Word on a daily basis.

At the same time, I became the matriarch of my family. I accepted the position wholeheartedly, looking forward to advise and comfort when needed. Furthermore, jobs began to open up to me, and the RN supervisor Wanda Bailey refused to allow me to retire completely. By that I mean, she always kept me working, which means I continued to earn income, even after the age of retirement, thereby sustaining a lifestyle to which I had grown accustomed.

Through it all, I heard Bishop's voice ringing in my ear, saying "Someone will use their power, their influence, and their ability to help you." His words proved to be true in my life. All around me, people were hearing good things about me and the word was getting back to me. That put a smile on my face because it was definitely a change from the past.

The new church environment that I was in was a new light in my life. I would go down to the church and help out of my own free will. That was something I would not have done before. During that season of my life, I embraced the ministry, God's people, society, and community work – trying to meet the needs of people around me.

In 2015, while in Arizona, God told me to read Joshua 1:8. He said, in three days you are going to possess the land. The victory is there!

Throughout my life, I have not won every battle, but I am determined to win the war! To me, that is what victory is all about.
If you have ever been in the valley, you have had a desire to travel to the mountain top! And once you get there, the thrust of life is so enjoyable. Then, you can say, "Look where He has brought me from," as you look down from the mountaintop. From there, you can go in and possess the land that the Lord God has given you to possess!

Lesson Learned

The most important lesson I could have learned is God will always have the last word!

He is the author and finisher of our faith.

He is in control of this universe, for He is the Great I Am.

He is our way maker.

He is the Alpha and the Omega.

He reigns supreme, and He is the Everlasting!

Oh, bless His name!

A Question to Ponder

Take a moment to reflect back over the last five or ten years of your life. Are you pleased with the choices you have made? Which choices please you and which disappoint you? Is there anything you can do to change any unpleasant situations you may be in? What plan of action can you take (with the Lord's guidance)?

_____

_____

_____

_____

_____

_____

_____

_____

_____

_____

_____

_____

_____

From the Valley to Victory!

About the Author

Audrey Pearl Williams has served in the capacity in Licensed Vocational Nurse for 35 years. She finds her career rewarding as it gives her an opportunity to give back the community.

She still has a love for traveling. She has visited Trinidad & Tobago, Mercedes & Nice, France, Montego, Monte Carlo, Pisa, Florence, Rome & Naples, Italy, Barcelona and Sabadell, Spain, Alaska, Canada, and Israel, which was the most rewarding.

She has a wealth of family to love and give her love in return, consisting of five children (one of whom is deceased), seventeen grandchildren, and sixteen great grandchildren.